COPY NO. 2

D1764904

Jill Magi's text-image projects document border-crossings between the body and public space, and between ideologies inscribed and experience as it is lived. Her projects combine research with the following forms: poetry, fiction, the essay, drawing, photography, and collage. She is the author of *SLOT* (forthcoming, Ugly Duckling Presse), *Torchwood* (Shearsman), *Threads* (Futurepoem), as well as the chapbooks *Furlough/Die for Love* (Ed. Press), *Poetry Barn Barn!* (2nd Avenue), *Cadastral Map* (Portable Press at Yo-Yo Labs), and numerous small, handmade books. Her essays have been anthologized in *The Eco-Language Reader* (Portable Press/Nightboat Books) and *Letters to Poets* (Saturnalia Books), and visual works have been exhibited at the Textile Arts Center, the Brooklyn Arts Council Gallery, the International Meeting of Visual Poetry, apexart, and Pace University. She is currently an artist-in-residence at the Textile Arts Center in Brooklyn, New York, and was a writer-in-residence with Lower Manhattan Cultural Council in 2006–07. Jill teaches at Goddard College and runs Sona Books, a chapbook press. For her small press work, she was recognized by *Poets & Writers Magazine* as one of the 50 most inspiring authors in 2010.

WITHDRAWN FROM THE POETRY LIBRARY

WITHDRAWN FROM THE PORTLY LIBRARY

Cadastral Map

Jill Magi

POETRY LIBRARY
SOUTHBANK CENTRE
ROYAL FESTIVAL HALL
LONDON SE1 8XX

Shearsman Books

Published in the United Kingdom in 2011 by
Shearsman Books Ltd
50 Westons Hill Drive
Bristol BS16 7DF

www.shearsman.com

ISBN 978-1-84861-172-6

Copyright © Jill Magi, 2005, 2011.

The right of Jill Magi to be identified as the author of this work
has been asserted by her in accordance with the
Copyrights, Designs and Patents Act of 1988.
All rights reserved.

Cover photo, and all photos in the text, are by the author.

Contents

This book is for my mother

Cadastral Map

shadow cast by text
or shadow-text come to light

pushing our paved roads
through the last silence then

What is Missing in the
Picture?

a whole world lying outside
the brackets returns to

haunt the narrowed
page

POETRY LIBRARY

a white thin cloud
at both ends of the book

numbers of pages have been
cut or torn out   flying

sunshiny shower my heart
originally

our hearts
and interleaved

thin pink
blotting paper still

there eighteen times
in odd spaces the word amen

Dear Sir,

The tree nodded to its fall
and the bird was flung from

her nest; and, though her
parental affection deserved

a better fate, was whipped down
by the twigs, which brought her

dead to the ground!
(Letter [   ])

foreboding dark melting
the mind produces

movement at the wildlife
viewing area over meadow

soft is the songbird
foregrounding a pregnant

forest (dusky conditions
being best)   Why Look at

Animals?   our wild mirror
nature written never

to return
to the soft illegible

[[   ]] initial
letters of

seventeen lines
left on the

stub
of the cut-out

page
[[   ]]

substantially
used

D.'s night-sky
description

in his poem [[   ]]
& [[   ]]

two or three
preliminary amens

to test the sharpened
end of her quill pen

timber vs.
trash-trees

roots
thatch

underbrush
vs. balance sheet

bedding
vines

row crops vs. weeds
saps for resins

kindling
hop poles

prose map   many pages
cut

a door and window tax
leads to fewer openings

a word
drops

to the bottom
into the central fold

of her notebook beneath
fodder mosses

Waldsterben
     he has

omitted this phrase and
the entire entry

if possibly I could escape
all other animals

I could not those of the
human kind

not knowing the way I must
perish in the woods

thus was I like the hunted
deer

hearing frequent rustlings
among the leaves

I at length
quitted the thicket

Dear Sir,

But the most abject reptile
and torpid of beings

distinguishes the hand that
feeds it, and is touched with

the feelings of gratitude!
(Letter XIII)

for fructification
havock among you

a border life
rabid and howling

cleare sunshine
of the gospel

fiery
flying serpents

to contemplate a tangled bank
one blends with the landscape

authoring nature
a language

whilst I read and write
pushing pen through

the last silence then

trees psalm-singing
the smoak lifted &

open'd this Romantick scene
I allowed myself, as I

sometimes do, to wander out
of myself

Divergence of Character
Ratio of Increase

The War of Nature
fear of Indian attack

discouraged the
projection

I can tell the wind is rising
the leaves trembling

on the trees
I can tell the wind is rising

the leaves trembling
on the trees

the wind blows from the
southeast corner of

hell but over my head
I see freedom in the air

the wind blows from the
southeast corner of

hell but over my head
I see freedom in the air

The West of which I speak is
but another name for Wild

The poets of the world will
be inspired by American

mythology
The Indian's trail to follow

the friendly and flowing
savage literature

attracts us   Very
sincerely yours,

Oh pleasure my constant walks
to find that Providence

should bestow such a
profusion of days

such a profusion of country
(from contra)

of nature (from
to be born) never

more than a simple surveyor
of land, I

pure wild glow of Heaven's
love is to bathe in spirit-

beams   green-winged   half-
cock antipode of paradise

tangled and gloomy forest
fowl-meadow grass

A Century of Dishonor   as if
we lived on the marrow of

koodoos devoured raw

Dear Sir,

In a district so diversified
as this, so full of hollow

vales and hanging woods, it
is no wonder that echoes

should abound! (Letter
XXXVIII)

between saw
and beheld

it is only just clear
that saw was the preferred

word   dull & misty
& grey very

rainy   sober starlight
evening   as much Jessamine

and honeysuckle
as could find room

to flourish   it made me
more than half tired

I was a poet
          copied out sonnets

for him
my head bad &

I lay long
[[   ]]

prairie big enough to carry
my eye clear to the sinking

rounding horizon a sentence
of charcoal on birchbark

written   Oh nature
rightly read a wind-harp

& we'll go nutting once more!
bird-while the loon laughed

long and loud   as the poet
must from time to time travel

the logger's path
and Indian trail

geography of hope   we simply
need it even if we never do

more than drive to its edge
and look in

for reassuring   America
tough as an Indian

this is the way to
learn the grammar of the

wild invisible   warning:
civilized man chokes his soul

as the heathen Chinese
their feet

I went forth into darkness
and rain   waiting

in the swamp lead by the
North Star   rice swamp

dank and lone   the fever-
demon strews poison

with falling dews   and made
my way into the woods

through bogs and briers
sickly sunbeams glare

learning to mark
the Editor's

of omission
among the trees & slips of

lawn   mountains enclosing
us round   she drew a full

line across the page after
each   slender note

of a remembered
redbreast

its boards covered
in mottled brown paper

the sky spread over
half-moon   the swallows

the garden the roses all
gently omitted

Dear Sir,

He therefore clipped the
hawk's wings, cut off his

talons, and, fixing a cork
on his bill, threw him down

among the brood-hens.
In a word, they never desisted

from buffeting their adversary
till they had torn

him in a hundred pieces!
(Letter XLIII)

poetico-trampo-geologist-bot.
and ornith-natural, etc!-!-!

rocks, trees, wind
on our cheeks!

the *solid* earth!
the *actual* world?

the *common sense!*
Contact! Contact!

Who are we? *where* are we?

Pray do not laugh at thus
seeing an artless countryman

tracing himself through
the simple modifications

of his life   For example
A Dutch farmer of Minisink

went to moving
with his Negroes

in his boots
a precaution

used to prevent
being stung

by The Enemies
of the Farmer

Dear Sir,

Timothy examines every wicket
and interstice in the fences

through which he will escape
if possible. The motives

that impel him to undertake
these rambles seem to be of

the amorous kind! (Letter
[   ])

sate in the house writing
in the morning while outdoors

vertical and slippery
the writing went back with him

on paths always under foot
her diary

(step not
                    upon the author)

open notebook
upon infrared inspection

revealed
no authorial presence

the rural suchness of land
having been uprooted

rashly

universal meter
a sentence

arrives at the summit over
common pasturage and there

disintegrates
her use of dashes quite

common (landscape vs.
brambles [diary]) without

composition
I planted it again

landscape archeology
panorama architecture

arrangements of affective
images is literature

a national consciousness
begins

when forest demanded an edge
so there his paths went

as the ex-cartographer found
ready employment in the

bustling colonies publishing
On the Situation,

Feelings, and Pleasures
of an American Farmer

fiscal legibility
pathway stress

vision
verstehen

sentence
survey

perfect-bound
property

the distinct downturn in our
literature from hope to

bitterness took place almost
at the precise time when the

frontier officially came
to an end,

in 1890

                         Very sincerely

yours,

Dear Sir,

The old tortoise, that I have
mentioned, presently, will be

under my eye and spending
more than two thirds of its

existence in a joyless
stupor. (Letter [   ])

HE: upon cutting open her
snake belly

found the abdomen
crowded with young

SHE: upon uprooting
felt as if I had been

committing an outrage
HE: which upon cutting open,

asked, which one to take?
and SHE: meditatively day

upon day writing
replanting not rashly

to have a drench of sleep
to note the blossoming

all by the road-side
oh drenching factoids my

Specimen Days and Collect
having distributed some

copies personally bound
remains a mystery still

her journals   (after
his

        editing

                  lost

)

POETRY LIBRARY

medicinal plant
marginalia erased

line-planted
Normalbaum

monoculture
centralized

forest floor nearly
weeded of hidden

transcripts as
seedling

story
survives the row

prose map lushly
precise and green

I look unto the hills from
whence cometh my help

from whence   cut open
description

named numbered thusly
inspired and partial

passive seemingly
was a foxglove

& the moon
came out

       suddenly
I lay in bed

having no
authorial presence

          I

               rashly

uprooted

A Curriculum for Boys

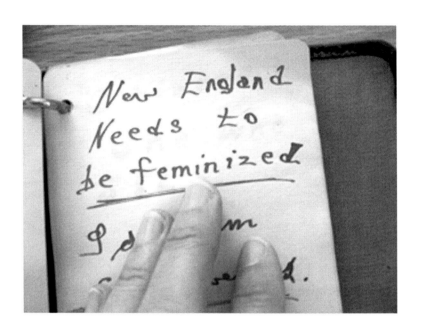

FOR THE COMMITTEE
ON THE TOPOGRAPHY AND CLIMATE

AGENDA: The battle of the wilderness
is still on unproductive hill farms all

pitted not against each other
but against time and space

(Vermont is The West
of New England)

A TOAST:
I have in mind the crest of the ridge

we will need some time
into every nook and corner

The Green Mountain Parkway
to penetrate

his marginalia
grab bag of PROGRESSIVE ideas

2. so that he who runs the ridge
may read the topography of the region

without undue distortion:
Barren and Rough Rivers

Treaty of Hard Labor
A point called Compromise

COMMISSION ON COUNTRY LIFE

5. (so that these Vermont hills may be happier
and easier to live with)

Remarks. Rocky
places. Name:

        yellow tape   drapes

                his

identifying

      her

and pictures. Coarse-toothed. Stubby
spur. Bare trees are not such a desolate

sight. Tracing
her last movements

      prickly brambles
at the bottom of winter.

Graves

Mark Graves, Tax Commissiner
New York State.

"Certainly, if your campaign
to beautify the highways results
in such pleasure to the eye
as your coloful map you will
indded have contributed much
to the happiness of mankind.
And I must say a-word about
your catch line "Radiant
Roadsides to Match Perfect
Pavements." Of a surety
nothing could be more appealing
to the imagination. I shall
watch with interest for the
article which accompanies the
map."

Feb. 26,929

seek your summer home
keep Vermont a secret

her historic scenic shrines
a state of mind and mountains

cohesive downtowns
come hither pamphlets

COMMITTEE ON SUMMER
RESIDENTS AND TOURISTS:

A) taking the waters
B) we have room to grow certainly

midweek
C) migration from Vermont

D) vs. the hippies
or the voluntary poor

E) NINETEEN HUNDRED AND
FROZE TO DEATH

Heartwellville
New Boston

Fair Haven
Pleasant Valley

Goose Green
(THE LURE OF HER SILENT PLACES)

Land title secret
(if it be wanting)

little spider web
(if it be wanting)

secret land of barley
(if it be wanting)

                    then satisfy!

We found false floors. Took measures
to arrest the sag. A staircase slopes

toward a serene arrival, a foyer, the brochure.
To vacate or land this history from a hilltop

changes. A vacation is not the shape of
settling.

Vein. Gland. Registers
make

great reading. Legend. Lobed,
without bristle-

    comb

        case
file. Tree-of-Heaven

    closed

        where another has been cut down.

Prickly Mountain
Total Loss Farm

drunken tipsy fence posts
trouble at Earth People's Park

RECREATIONAL SHOPPING
CULTURAL HERITAGE TOURISM

(they may say they want to stay on a farm
but I bet they'd rather stay next to one)

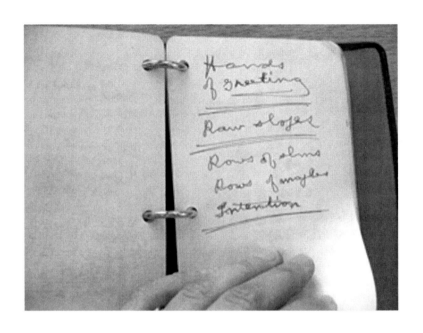

Fort number 4. Site number 2. Found
on or close to bedrock. Sectioned

sifted proof. Shallow grave, shadowy
birch. Hide the baby

in knotty bark. Owl wings
     wind   ghosted

no longer on vacation
a nation comes upon

a rusting gate   a railroad
traces. Red maple. Mossycup oak.

Driving toward her farm
found in a field

   hummingbird drawn to anything red
Last seen

   means wedge-shaped. Is with fine teeth
twigs hairless or nearly so. No.

    Yes.   Yes.

        No.

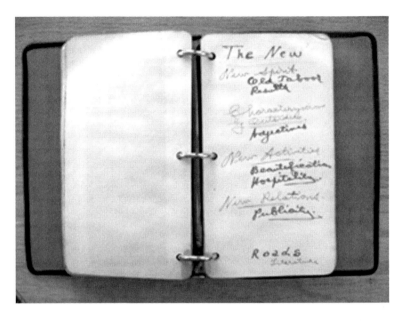

To retire submarginal lands and
valley-mindedness   away

with dead trees and lifeless
branches   bad sign placement

(CONCERNING CHARTS 1–10)
he pushed his boat out onto the lake

and there died
debating indigenous attractions

vs. artificial   all cities cemented
together against THE SEVEN ROADSIDE SINS:

                    Vermont sieves slowly anyway

as the she-bear rears her cub
in the depths of virgin forests these

she wants
her friends

in other states
to come

within her
borders

her ways
are ways

of simplicity
yet sincere

cordiality
she charms she

offers nothing
pretentious!

Undersides mostly velvety. She
loved the outdoors.

This is the key to trees
in leafy condition. Severe

blow to the

to trees in leaf-less condition. Where blazing
has faded, heart-shaped

from the beginning. Leaf scars

recovered in a wooded area. Crack willow

carefully pressed. Downplaying
the threat   a very careful person

red rose still tries to flower and body therein found

leave your porch light on

Pictures should be painted with trees and
shrubs and flowers and ferns

whereas other states have a mega-attraction
MADAM,

IT IS YOUR MUD!

                    MY CREED OF THE OUT OF DOORS:
1. all good Vermonters should leave home

2. the pastoral vacation outdistanced
all other kinds of tourism

5. one sixth federal parkway land or
6. money for flood control

7. at that point you will lose the brand and
8. the whole matrix will collapse, signed,

LANDSCAPE   PROGRESS   PUBLICITY

                              (A CURRICULUM FOR BOYS)

To touch the serenity of a clear blue
laminated map   roped is a room

through a doorway tightly seen
the framed clink of antiques, her

smooth modern highways beckon you onward
as that's when the warblers are going through

               A CONTINUOUS NATURAL PARK!

the personal impact
of a failed plan

and lost vote

             take my boat, take my boat, take my boat

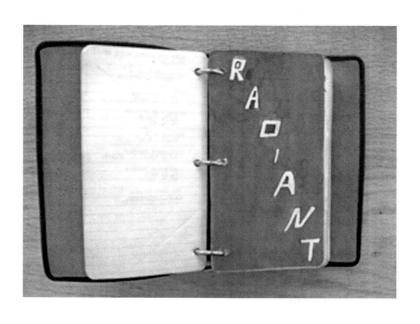

Hawk's Got a Chicken and Gone

epicenter
esker

fold
marl

price supports
molds

test holes
price controls

depression acting
as hinge line

cracking basement rock
pillow lava

       hawk's got a chicken
and gone

hawk's got
a chicken and gone

[interruption in taping] the interviewer, hmm
and in that family history laying there

hmm, mother and daddy have a copy,
the farmer [touches microphone]

just a boxed house
[inaudible] you'd generally had some thorn trees

round it
was a little town known as Wide Awake

and generally there was a good many
rock on it

and there was a missionary lady
come up

and the dirt washed off the hill land
so all that was lost

(stalks would get taller
leaves would get longer

leaves would get broader
started out with the spouge

and then the lugs)
somebody invited her up

(then the bright leaf
the red leaf and then the tips)

so all that was lost [sound of truck noise]
over to Lee County and on down to Primrose

was a missionary lady
don't know why she come up

You may view graphs and tables
of coal production by county

You may view farmers
as they crop the narrow bottoms

and navigate the ridges
to pasture their cattle and hogs

in the woods
where resources are shallow and

allowed to collapse   You may view
[inaudible] a cancer belt by county

Singing, I'm sorry darlin cause you let me down,
a truer love now you think you've found

But when I'm laid deep down in the ground,
you're gonna be sorry you let me down

I believed you darlin when you said to me that we'd be
          happy,
that we'd be free. But now I've

found, dear, a fault in thee, when we were wed,
love, I could not see

POETRY LIBRARY

well we went to the grades
and that was it

and you could say I like pretty lumber
yes sir pretty well

my favorite being the poplar, says
it grows up straight

umhmm, the interviewer
[inaudible] oh, the bean

is easy grown, says
[interruption in taping]

Come upon the heaped stones of a chimney
Come seekers of quick wealth in timber

and ore. Come gas tapped for company profits
and free heat for whomever on the land

but not the profit. She keeps switches of her own
hair for a wig just in case

Singing, last night the pale moon was shining,
last night when all was still,

I was wandering alone in sadness, out among
the woodland hills. I heard the birds

a-singing out among the trees and dew
and all the birds, my darling, were singing

were singing of you

was something by the name of bluing
she says

hmm, the interviewer
was said to make 'em whiter

says hmm
that you blued your clothes [chuckle]

still a rough setting, a rough job,
the farmer

we'd go in and help him out maybe to set
his crop, yes I've done that many of a day

and the babies they slept with their mother
and we washed on the board

Rough
Creek

Graben
Chevron

Subsurface
Peak

Energy
Rome

Trough
Consortium

Big
Lime

Project
Equitable

and the farmer got the least wage
and who slept where, the interviewer asks

well, says the farmer
we let it wilt a little bit [chuckle]

then spread it on the patch
been long tore down, the farmer

hauled it on a horse-drawn sled or
the way nature comes up, says the farmer

tell 'em about the end of his tie
[interruption in taping] was shot

clean off
shot clean off?

but we had love
not much but love

but there would be sixty people and oh,
the collection would be about eleven cents

[inaudible] yes, was narrow leaf tobacco
and it was [Twist Bud?] and [Killian?]

asks the interviewer, was [Julia Pride?]
and Golden Burley and the farmer says,

so you lay it off in rows
umhmm, says the interviewer

and you let it lay a little while
or come a big heavy snow

[inaudible] and plenty of rocks
pulls the young trees crooked

They say she'll need treatments
and from below it looks as if a giant knife

cut the state in two. A blooming thicket
used to be a doorway and the old road

adhered to the ridge until the bypass
came through. You may download all coal

production statistics in spreadsheet format.
You may be near to the sleep of things,

great compactions underneath, listening
to the women report on recoveries

before a coming night chill slices
through the valley of the creek

Singing, so bury me underneath the willow,
under the weeping willow tree,

so that he may know where I am sleeping
and perhaps he'll weep for me

and the ones who lived to get grown
was raised up on a hillside

and feed the stock, says the farmer
the stock, the interviewer repeats

no that's not a real strong memory,
and made cottage cheese

from the clabber milk
or they grew up and made teachers

the interviewer, or the ones with money
bought the blackberries

us, we picked 'em, the farmer
I see, the interviewer

Marrowbone
Viper

War-Branch
Sourwood Mountain

distressed
counties

Antepast
Bledsoe

hewed-stone
schoolhouse

the problem
of spelling

absentee
landlords

Dear Miss New Jersey,

A large Indian settlement existed in Huntsville
prior to its settlement,

writing

                        no fences would be used
for the purpose of supplying the troops

Sincerely,
General George Washington

(to discover items of the past after the spring
thaws!)

What will happen to the first tranquil views?

from fingers fall hair long pulled
from a brush past thistles for birds

for their nests, he says
that the truth will spring out of the earth

and that leaves decay under rocks bare
trees in November silver-light

mall lights crackle on at dusk, looking
for a space to park

a bag of tomatoes from Great Meadows
up the basement stairs a trail of red

their split skins spill where
settlest the furrows   where hands

stained near-black
from the muck, Miss New Jersey,

this is fine, snowing tiny parachutes
seeds as soft comes the edge of the woods

the entrance of words   satiny blue
sneakers under my colonial gown calico

the Bicentennial parades a Miss New Jersey
town of mock-settlers marching

a bobby pin works loose from a bonnet and
he holds a pitchfork in the family portrait

of immigrants   disappointed
by the fireworks fogged over   we live here

New Jersey, fleeing as a bird to your
mountain   surveyor's tape flaps

from our red-tailed hawk circling
this is the Doppler Effect   Away

in a Manger   Amazing
Grace

to the right, note
the few rock shelters

known to be used by the early
Indians

who moved through
the area, first as a frontier

secondly as a typical American
farming village, who left

lynchings at the intersection
scalpings   while Jenny jumped to escape

the Indians   I finger-trace maps
on my lap the story underneath legend and key

she
she

SHADES OF DEATH ROAD

shadow-shape of county lines as golden
grows the noon there (here) were 400 slaves

Did You Know? as the pamphlet defines
a girl   perspectives echo between

mile-markers   underground
railroad stop and hid in caves here

(there) we imagined tunnels
and called it SHADES for short

to see as an artist but it's not practical,
Miss New Jersey

to look at the shades of gray and brown
the winter clearing now a deeper forest

cold smell   taste of snow
on evergreens   lightning bugs meadow

cast lightning upon the willows
to establish distance

count between flash
and clap

97. A Red Oak ab't 1 ½ foot diameter.
The ground descends part Northerly and part N. Easterly.

At 37 a Grassy Pond 6 ch. wide and ab't 40 long; bears ab't N.E.;
an old beaver dam ab't 10 ch. below;

S.W. a branch of Pequest called Allamuche.
98. A Red Oak in a small plain ab't 16 Inches diameter,

60 L. East of the line. At 67 branch of Pequest,
runs ab't 30 W. and ab't 30 L. wide.

99. A White Oak stake in a plain on the N. side
of a large Branch of Pequest. At 16 ch. the N. edge of

a plain, the Mountain begins. 100. An Ash Sapling
on the N. side of some low swampy ground.

Left off the prose map
and went to a house belonging to Rich Green.

by right angles to Ghost Lake
Quakers followed property

lines settled into No
Trespassing   hollow-point bullet

empty dime bag atop the gentle
crackle of gravel   Posted & Patrolled

beaver pole shavings
trapped

fog
slips between states of develop

or preserve
blue marker memory of limestone

shelter   damp leaves
lean-to between loam and looming

chip and tar vectors toward
a house   used to be our walls shifted

up, down
modern

swath of earth now cut
mounted by a new colonial   still

ground thaw
won't absorb flood waters

valley lined
by disfigured rock walls

pre-dated our idea of
nestledness

lost,

                    we

write it down
right off

Heller Road in case
around blind

turns

                mirrors

in shallow water social
science is about the thirteen colonies

and crayfish trolling beneath
the hiss of a hunter's arrow

burrs on my socks
windbreakers snag berry bushes

                        milkweed pod, pull it
open

           this is a fine thing to do

in fall another casing plastic or
white silk there flying soft   soft

find the tag slashed in red always
always, Miss New Jersey, never never

pay full price first check the back
racks, she says

dim pat of leather gloves
against the steering wheel

blinker ticks turning up and down
rows looking for a space and that leaves

decay
smell of corn stalks

cut sharp a labyrinth beneath moonlight
in the season of not silent

the owl who perched
on our metal gutters scratching

field-yelling crows and a mockingbird
calls   marble   another

dead Stuyvesant
flung open and rusting

mansion gates a search
for the slave quarters

foundations end here
dead woodpecker at my feet returning

to make grave rubbings a sooty
history if the paper is large enough

for the historical marker in metal relief
cold history mounts the partial

                    or were abolitionists
while we learned to spell

you don't tarry
at the cemetery

our push toward the west
of the state   a private forest

and two-car garage   the fruitful
trees and cedars

plots
cut the valley

shingles painted beige a tasteful shade
spacious and sliding

glass doors to a deck on the back
rather than a porch to watch or say

                            a line of transplants
prevents a clear view

a well-groomed rural
has been written

its setting
a tranquil

      (skirmishes

skirmishes

                skirmishes)

I sat on the rock at the base of the hill
in the crook of the turn declaring

that I would become a naturalist
as cars slowed down to see if I was alright

writing "Dear Miss New Jersey,
Come on out!

Watch the pigs at Ervey Farm and count
the chipmunks   walk in rows of corn

grab at clusters of Queen Anne's lace
do the buttercup test   those croaking frogs

equal bad weather approaching so come,
look at my quilting!"

The Meander (an Essay)

The cadastral map is drawn as if from an aerial view, composed by surveyors to determine land ownership for the purpose of taxation. The cadastral map does not indicate where the land is fertile, swampy, or rocky. It does not indicate knolls, forests, valleys. Nor does it express the collaboration and exchange between farmers or those who move through the land. Its lines respect one purpose, one knowledge: state-sponsored commoditization.

I enter as a writer, one kind of mapmaker, needing to ask, is traditional nature writing in English a cadastral map? Abstracting, narrowing, taking an especially strong hold in North America, the New World that never was new? Even as "green is the new black" and environmentalism gains moral momentum, is "nature writing" still our flawed point of origin, creating ideas of the land and nature that tend to erase people and local knowledge as we go?

With an ear to this ground, my research began and source texts emerged: Gilbert White's 18th century *The Natural History and Antiquities of Selborne*, de Crèvecoeur's *Letters from an American Farmer* and *Sketches of Eighteenth Century America*, Mary Rowlandson and Cotton Mather, Ralph Waldo Emerson and Henry David Thoreau, John Muir, Charles Darwin, Wallace Stegner. Then came the meander—the force of water that defies the traditional riverbed: ground-level knowledge and the people are never erased and they are, thankfully, willful. These "meandering" source texts included Dorothy Wordsworth's journals—her diary entries (unruly brambles) contrast the poet-hero's groomed and revised landscapes. Similarly, against the texture of taxonomy is Walt Whitman's loping anti-expertise of *Specimen Days and Collect*. Crucially, there is Elizabeth Cook-Lynn's *Why I Can't Read Wallace Stegner*; the narratives of Olaudah Equiano and Frederick Douglass: all three make legible the institutions of slavery and genocide at the center of the history of North

American land, profits, language, pollutions, and even notions of "conservation."

A policy is a path that is made, an effect to feel. Into my research came the journals and notes of James Taylor, progressive policy-maker who built a 20th century idea of Vermont similar to that state's 19th century "come hither pamphlets," solidifying "the two Vermonts": playground for the upper classes and site of struggle for the Northern Appalachian poor. The instructive irony of his simultaneous desire to present nature (read: conserve) and build a parkway right through the middle of it. Vermonters, more interested in spending state funds on flood relief, voted no on the parkway.

In contemporary Appalachia, I noted the oral historian's problem of spelling. I heard the local farmer's audible skepticism that links, in ecological instinct, "transcript" with "erasure;" a fierce and playful poetry in their speech. In Kentucky, I listened to women tell stories of illness and I thought of mining, toxicities, absentee landlords in the form of multi-national corporations, and local struggles for dignity.

Finally, I remember my childhood in New Jersey's dairy farm country: our move "out to the country." We were a long line of city and suburban dwellers seeking peace, space. When I was about ten years old I found an arrowhead in a freshly plowed field, took it home, and propped it up against the spines of my childhood books. I walked the aisles of the supermarket and imagined the fossilized footsteps of the Lenni Lenape Indians—their authoring marks—underneath the erasure of concrete floors.

A focus on meticulous recycling, emissions standards, and other single-issue lobbying efforts (and legal gains too insignificant to impede the disaster), might be evidence that certain mapmakers remain largely invisible and therefore powerful. How the lack of universal health care, poverty, joblessness, the need for campaign-finance reform *are* environmental concerns. I have a suspicion that some powerful eyes are happy to watch us squabble over whether or not to use paper to make books and about whose household is more "earth-friendly." Another puritanical inheritance: an over-developed desire to judge one another, alongside a too-fierce individualism, and the anxious need to do something, anything (often simplifying the complex) without studying up (endangered intellectual work).

Still, I crave a walk in the woods. Poetry meanders its way away from this essay—and toward The Psalms: "I look unto the hills from whence cometh my help."

At every turn, degrees of legibility, a focus that comes in and out, position-depending. Don't look away. Listen, there is history. Earth and bones beneath your map give weight back with each authoring step.

Additional Sources and Thanks

Research for this project in New Jersey, Vermont, and Kentucky was supported by a grant from the Professional Staff Congress of the City University of New York. The 'Cadastral Map' section was published in 2005 as a chapbook by Portable Press at Yo-Yo Labs. Other portions of the book have appeared in *HOW2*, *CutBank Poetry*, *the tiny*, and *Tarpaulin Sky*. Thanks to those editors for their support. Thanks to Jennifer Firestone for her careful read of the manuscript along the way. Thanks to Ellen Baxt, Joanna Sondheim, and Johannah Rodgers for feedback on the project during its early stages.

I want to thank Jean Magi for providing lay histories of northern New Jersey, including *A History of Green Township* by Thomas J. Beirne, a text from which some of the poems in 'Dear Miss New Jersey,' originate.

For information on the history of land use and public policy in Vermont, I am grateful to Trina Magi and the librarians at the Bailey/Howe Library of the University of Vermont. I also want to thank Paul Carnahan at the Vermont Historical Society Library for directing me to the notebooks and archive of James Taylor. The photos in this book are from that archive, and many of the poems in 'A Curriculum for Boys' begin with language found in his archive.

Thanks to Lois Webster Woosley and the entire Messer family for research in Kentucky. In 'Hawk's Got a Chicken and Gone,' some poems are inspired by language from the University of Kentucky Oral History Collection, especially from the Family Farm Oral History Project. Other inspirations include traditional mountain and coal songs, language from coal and gas company Web sites, and an essay by Wendell Berry.

Theoretical underpinnings for this manuscript come, in part, from James Scott's essay 'Nature and Space' in his *Seeing Like a State: How Certain Schemes to Improve the Human Condition Have Failed*. David Mazel's essay, 'American Literary Environmentalism as Domestic Orientalism' in *The Ecocriticism Reader: Landmarks in Literary Ecology*, was foundational. Two articles on the failings of environmentalism, available on the Web, were also important: Michael Shellenberger and Ted Nordhaus' 'The Death of Environmentalism' and the 'The Soul of Environmentalism,' by the 'Redefining Progress' think-tank based in Oakland, California.

Lightning Source UK Ltd.
Milton Keynes UK

178540UK00001B/5/P